A IS FOR Aesthetic

THE INSTAMAMA ABCs

written by Hannah Johnson and Jacalynn Sokolow

A is for Aesthetic

The golden rule of the 'gram.
Posting pretty pictures
So carefully planned.

B is for Babies

And bonnets and bumps.
The cute moments that make
Instamamas' hearts jump!

C is for Coffee

Our sweet morning fuel.
Add latte art to make it
Optimally cool.

D is for Diaper Bag

The instamama's tool kit.
The bigger the better,
So all our stylish gear fits.

E is for Earth Tones

Olive and beige are a must!
And don't forget the answer
Is never really 'not rust.'

F is for Flatlays

And fiddle leaf ferns.
The more that you post these,
The more likes that you'll earn.

G is for Giveaway

Run! Tag your friends!
And tell your partner you won it
When they ask how much you spent.

H is for Hashtags

Add as many as you please!
And don't forget us,
Tag #instamamaABCs

I is for Influencer

They live the glamorous life.
Showing their followers how to be
The perfect instamama and wife.

xxx_xxxx

1,032 Posts   **1.3M** Followers   **2 352** Following

Xxx Xxxx
Our days captured

J is for Jumpsuits

Yes they're back in style.
As long as they're linen,
They are just so versatile.

K is for Kiddos

Our sweet little muses,
Who cooperate with pictures
When he or she chooses.

L is for Letterboard

There's no need to shout!
Be it milestones or sarcasm,
Just spell it all out!

M is for Moses Baskets

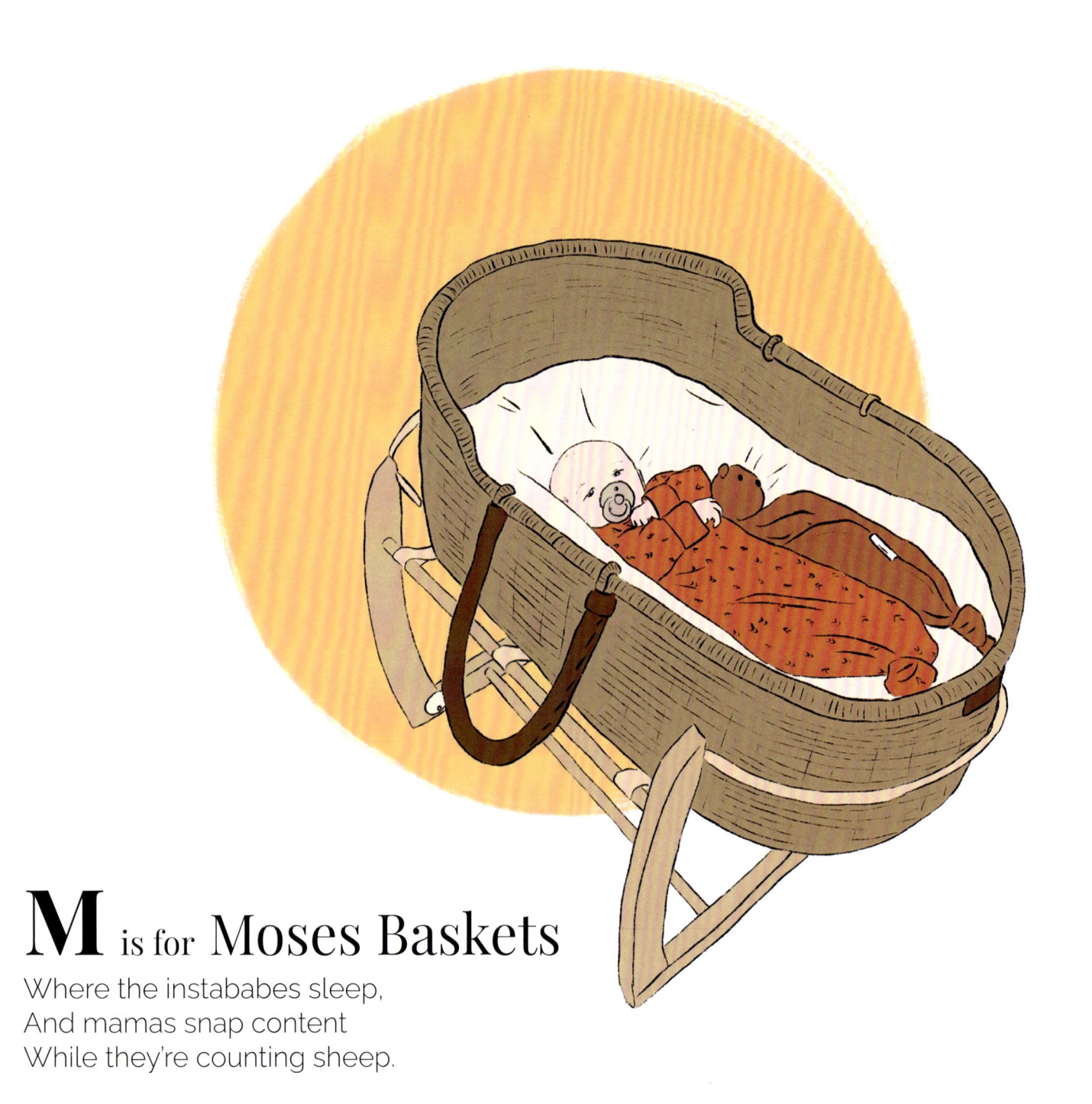

Where the instababes sleep,
And mamas snap content
While they're counting sheep.

N is for Nature

So get outdoors with the fam.
But don't forget to take pictures
To post on the 'gram!

O is for Outfits

New clothes that make us feel great.
And if posted with baby,
Then they'd best coordinate.

P is for Postpartum

That magical time
Of fresh baby snuggles
And being too tired to rhyme.

Q is for Quiet

Snuggly pictures in bed...
Unless you have toddlers,
Then quiet fills you with dread!

R is for Ring Sling

Our favorite babywearing tool.
A piece of linen and two rings
That makes a mama look cool.

S is for (Insta)stories

So tell us what's new with you.
Food, outfits, and playtime!
Please post that daily review.

T is for Travel

Whether seaside or mount.
If you didn't 'gram it,
Did it even count?

U is for Unboxing

Show off that new gear!
And let your followers know
To "Swipe up right here!"

V is for Vibes

Only good ones allowed.
So stop all the shaming
And make mama proud!

W is for Wooden

Both decor and toys.
There'll be no bright plastic
For these girls and boys.

X is for (e)Xtra

Yes we're over the top.
But that's #momlife
So no we won't stop!

Y is for Yoga

And not just the pants.
So get out your mat
And give down dog a chance.

Z is for Zodiac

The Instamom's pickup line.
Just add enneagram type
And tell me your number and sign.

A, B
Kirsten Saldana

Kirsten is a graphic designer, specializing in digital illustrations and pattern design. She loves to bring art to life on physical goods. Her biggest joy is raising her little boy in Venice, California. Follow her on Instagram **@sweetsoulshop.co**.

C, D
Mikenzi Jones

Mikenzi is a graphic designer, illustrator and photographer. She's raising two boys in North Carolina where they love spending their days in nature, finding new adventures and being creative. You can check out her art **@kenzistudioco**.

E, F
Aurelia Ugarte

Aurelia lives in Jacksonville, Alabama with her husband & two children. She runs a restaurant, has her hands in many crafts, thrifts, and loves styling. To see more into her life, check out her insta **@ugarteaurelia**.

G, H
Ashli McAllister

Ashli lives in Virginia Beach, VA with her husband and two children. When she's not chasing her little ones, you can find her painting surfboards, drawing portraits, or eating pasta. To see more of her work, check out **@ashlimarierose**.

I, J
Piyarat Mukura

Piyarat lives in beach town in Thailand called Pattaya with her husband and daughter. She's a Visual Art graduate. Capturing people and their connections has always been her passion. Check out her work **@mamamoonmuse**.

K, L
Tayler Wooten

Tayler hails from Nashville and has spent time as an illustrator and studied animation. He tattoos for a living, and enjoys spending his time with his beautiful wife and kiddos. Checkout more of his creations on Instagram **@taylerwooten**.

M, N
Kara Tinsley

Kara lives in Dallas, Texas with her fiancé and two children. She is a full time stylist and work from home mom and part-time freelance illustrator. Check out more of her life on Instagram **@karatinsley**.

O, P
Marissa O'Leary

Marissa lives in New York with her husband and two daughters. She was a preschool teacher, now a stay at home mom and part time illustrator. To see more of her work check her out on Instagram **@olearydesigns**.

Q, R
Whitney Anderson

Whitney lives in Dalton, Georgia with her husband and three children. She's a SAHM that loves delving into her creative side and paints when she finds the time! You can check out her work on Instagram **@sunshineandpine**.

S, T
Sara Bertrand

Sara is a mom of four girls living in the French Riviera. She enjoys creating in every way - from sewing to baking to portraiture. You can follow her colourful life on insta **@bisousbiche**.

U, V
Lauren Helms

Lauren is an artist, mom, and wife living on the coast of Connecticut. Since her twins extremely premature birth she has advocated for families like hers to get the resources and understanding they need to thrive. You can find her blend of humor and advocacy work **@TheCrazyHairedMomma**.

W, X
Dan Sandoval

Daniel lives in Arizona with his wife and two kids. He is a full time director of animation, but has worked as a designer and a photographer as well. He illustrates at all times of the night to fuel his creative outlet. To see more of his work check him out on Instagram: **@robotfeelings**.

Y, Z
Anna Devlin

Anna lives just outside Atlanta, Georgia with her husband and three children. She is a social worker turned SAHM who spends her nap times drawing, painting and creating. Follow her work on Instagram **@anna.devlin.art**.

Hannah Johnson & Jacalynn Sokolow

Hannah lives with her small but mighty family in Chicago. Most days, you can find her helping the team at Vios Fertility Institute create families. Outside of work, she's an avid traveler, Peloton enthusiast, occasional yogi, and explorer of all her great city has to offer. Say hello and follow along as she navigates motherhood and life **@habejo**.

Jacalynn lives with her tiny circus in Baltimore. She is a pediatric nurse turned SAHM and apparently now book author. Other titles include house plant hobbyist, donut connoisseur, perpetual redecorator and midnight painter. To see more of her adventures, check out **@thesidewayshouse** and **@shepaintsbystars**.

Hannah and Jacalynn were brought together through new motherhood, babywearing, and the wild and wacky world of internet mom groups. Both enjoy hopping on planes to meet online friends, all things babies, and are self-confessed, unashamed Instamamas.